Ready, Set, Deal

*How a small minority- and women-owned company
can win big business from Corporate America*

Rengen Li

Because of the dynamic nature of the Internet, any web addresses or links contained in this book may have changed since publication and may no longer be valid. The views expressed in this work are solely those of the author and do not necessarily reflect the views of the publisher, and the publisher hereby disclaims any responsibility for them.

Any people depicted in stock imagery provided by Thinkstock are models, and such images are being used for illustrative purposes only.
Certain stock imagery © Thinkstock.

Lulu Publishing Services rev. date: 09/30/2014

Contents

Dedication

This booklet is dedicated to millions of small minority- and women-owned enterprises (MWBEs) in the United States of American.

To Lin Zhao, who, for more than 30 years, has encouraged, coached, pushed me to be better.

Disclaimer

I admire minority and women business owners. You have so many obstacles and barriers but you persist and succeed. You are my inspiration. Over the years, I have been blessed to meet, know, and become personal friends with so many of you. One time I felt very flattered when someone said that I was "blackened." I wrote these pages as a testimony that I have learned so much from you. If these pages can offer some help to a new minority and women business enterprise (MWBE) or give some reminders to a more experienced MWBE, I will be excited and happy.

All the stories I talk about in the following pages are true – but to protect privacy, I have changed names of businesses, their owners, and in many cases, their products as well. If you see something similar to your experience, please don't jump into conclusions right away. In almost all cases, that particular story took place multiple times. You might or might not be one of these times. I use these stories to make the pages easy to read and to illustrate a point or two. To borrow a standard statement, "All characters appearing in this work are fictitious. Any resemblance to real persons, living or dead, is purely coincidental."

Also, I used the BigCo as a representation of your big corporate customer. It does not mean my employer, The Coca-Cola Company, or any other specific corporation. Where I can name the company, I stated as such. If it says BigCo, it is a representative of a big corporation.

Lsatly, all views in this book are mine and I take full responsibility for them. These views don't represent those of my former and current employers nor do they represent any of the advocacy organizations whose boards I used to serve or am currently serving. I do hope that after reading the following pages, they would agree with me and make some changes in how they operate their business or organizations.

Preface

During my tenure as a supplier diversity professional, I met thousands of minority and women business owners. Though some were very successful in doing business with corporations and had revenues in the hundreds of millions, many were rather small and most were from one to ten million dollars in revenue. One thing stroke me the most. Almost all of these companies, big or small, used the same approach in selling to Fortune 500 companies. They all went to the same tradeshows and conferences and met with the same supplier diversity managers. During that time, I had seen too many triumphs that were not repeated and too many lessons not learned but got repeated.

How could we do better and produce more results through the conferences and tradeshows? A few of us, in addition to sharing drinks and war stories, argued, debated, and explored from different angles. For me, the solutions could come from different ways. Certainly, the advocacy organizations such as the regional minority supplier development councils and WBENC affiliates could do more innovative programs. One of the most important aspects to me, though, was to enhance the MWBEs' capabilities. I started presenting some of the thinking and learning at tradeshows and conferences. March of 2010, I was invited to give a keynote speech at the International Business Summit in Tampa, Florida, organized by a coalition of bi-country chambers. My proposition, "Stop Networking and Start Dealmaking," was very well received by the international audience. That gave me more courage to write down some of the stories and lessons.

Then one day in the Spring of 2014, I had a lunch with an executive coach, Nancy Lewis, and she challenged me to put together what I have written and publish the book within two months. Without that push, this book would be still in my Dropbox! (I also learned how a coach should work.) Thank you, Nancy.

I would like to express my sincere appreciation to Cece Webster, then VP of Procurement for Coca-Cola North America. In the Summer of 2000, she gave me the opportunity to be a supplier diversity manager, even though I had no experience in strategic procurement, nor did I have heard minority and women owned business or "supplier diversity." I specially want to call this out, because I believe there are too many procurement managers and business executives who are too risk-averse. I would encourage them to provide opportunities to MWBEs when there is a reasonable chance that they will be successful. With little bit more help, support, and mentoring, many MWBEs will thrive.

I would also want to thank Ms. Johnny Booker, former supplier diversity executive at The Coca-Cola Company. She taught me more than supplier diversity. Her experience, her dedication, her commitment were exemplary and made the difference. Her willingness to take a stand and upset people for the right cause has proved to be her great leadership asset. We all loved her many life stories and wit ("Common senses are not common practices;" "Keep your antenna up 24/7;" "Rising tide lifts all boat" are examples).

During my 10-year career in supplier diversity, many friends and colleagues in the circle, who selflessly shared their experience and thought leadership with me, and who mentored and coached me and gave me opportunities to join various boards and to contribute. Michael and Michelle Robinson, Patricia Richards, Valerie Nesbitt, Fritz Valsaint, Cathy Holmyer, Roby Paton, Stacey Key, Malik Ali, Al Richardson, Fernando Hernandaz, Rosemary Jones, Debbie Stone, Joan Kurr, Reggie Layton, Reggie Williams, Susan Au Allen, Kay Tyson, Karmetria Dunham Burton, Vanessa Bull, Ken Huff, Craig Hardin, Ying McGuire, and many many others. Credits also go to many of my colleagues at The Coca-Cola Company including many business leaders and procurement professionals who were our champions in supplier diversity such as Chris Horrace, Dana Hasson, Kevin List, Ann Moren, Meg Dooley, Rick Callahan, Tuffy Williams, Tracy Rivers, and John Lewis. Thank you and you are the real heroes.

I want to also thank to my editor, Betsy Rhame-Minor, for her careful editing and suggestions to make it readable and consistent.

Last and the most important, I want to thank again to all those minority- and women-owned business enterprises I have had the pleasure and honor to meet and learn from.

Introduction

To get business from Corporate America successfully, a minority- and women-owned business owner must treat it a strategic decision, employ a deliberate process, and have some luck. The small MWBE must be ready in many aspects of the business enterprise, know and execute marketing, and only then can he or she go for the prize. In the following pages, I share many successes and failures I have witnessed as a supplier diversity professional in working with small diversity firms and my reflections on how MWBEs can be even more successful.

My hunch is that many minority and women owned firms have launched their pursuit for corporate business too early. If you are not making it on your own with your existing customers, it may be premature for you to join in the hunting trip. Get your stuff ready first – including gears, supplies, and of course, a GPS.

The tidbits are roughly in three categories: get ready before you jump in; go for the prize; and grow your business. There are many more stories to be told, successes shared, and lesson learned. If one of these pages can help one MWBE be more successful, I have met my objective.

Make the Leap

Sunil Patel owned a small IT consulting company. He had been very supportive of BigCo's effort in the local area to bring more Asian American businesses to its supply chains, but Sunil had not been active in working with BigCo in other regions. Many of his peers and friends went to tradeshows nationwide, but he declined BigCo's invitation to attend a tradeshow on the West Coast. Sunil explained that he supported the events in his city because he felt he needed to support the community. But, he was actually not ready to do big business with corporations and therefore, it would not be a good investment of his time or money to attend tradeshows outside the state. The supplier diversity manager at BigCo appreciated his honesty and stopped inviting him or anyone who was not ready yet.

Sunil was right. Doing business with large corporations is not for everyone. Even if everyone else is doing business with the Wal-Marts or Coca-Colas of the world, that does not mean you should necessarily do the same. While there are many benefits to doing business with large corporations, it can kill your business if you're not careful. Big corporations ask a lot, don't want to pay much, and pay you late.

In most cases, selling to the big corporations will produce smaller margins for you, particularly if you are in the commodity business. More often than not, when you are coming either as an addition or replacement to an incumbent vendor, the corporate customer has the benefit of comparing prices. They know the actual cost. As a result, you cannot charge larger margins. If your operation is not efficient, you may end up losing instead of making money.

Big corporations ask a lot from you: quality product, quality service, and timely delivery. Depending on your area of expertise, they may ask for big insurance coverage. To a small company, it can be hard to understand, but to a large business, liability is one of the biggest risks. One time, a minority business entrepreneur (MBE) got a contract with BigCo to do a small IT project, and BigCo's risk management group insisted the small MBE should carry $5 million in liability insurance. For a major corporation, the size of the project is irrelevant, because any small mistake can cause millions of dollars in damages, and some can be beyond monetary terms. It turned out that the insurance cost for a $5 million policy would be larger than the contracted value. Similarly, many companies ask a second tier vendor to provide the same level of insurance as a first tier supplier, or the first tier vendor would demand the same level of insurance from its second tier vendors. Is it fair? No. But your corporate customer has to protect itself. So before you decide to sell to big corporations, you have to think about what it means before you jump in.

Payment terms can also hurt you. Today, if you have a 30-day payment term, you should celebrate. Since 2008's recession, many corporations now ask for 60-day, 90-day, or even 120-day terms. If you don't have a solid cash flow or a revolving credit line, the payment term alone could ruin your business.

Major corporations tend to hold grudges and are much less forgiving. If you fail on the first try, they seldom give you a second chance. The reason is that the corporate personnel have become more and more risk-averse; they don't want to take on any more risk than they have to. In addition, the buyers at major corporations don't want to be blamed for supply problems. These people have so many contracts to work on, they don't like any problems, period. Their mantra is that if it is not broken, don't fix it. That's why it is very difficult for a new vendor to come in.

I hope that these and many other drawbacks of doing business with big corporations don't deter you from doing so. I just want to make a point that it should be a strategic decision on your part. Doing business with big corporations can be one of the most effective ways to grow your business, but think before you jump.

What Business are You In?

A couple of years ago, I had a lawn service company managing my yard, mowing the grass, and trimming the bushes. Their service started all right, but deteriorated over time. Every week, I had to check and see whether the lawn care people came or not. If not, I had to do something about it. So I decided to replace them. I talked to a couple of companies that service my area. Scott, the owner of a smaller firm, told me that he had been in the lawn care business for 28 years and his folks were all "professional."

Scott's comments got me thinking. What was I looking for? Was I looking for a "professional" or "expert" lawn mower and a bush trimmer or something else? Over the years, I had learned how to mow and edge the lawn and how to trim bushes. I was not an expert at all, and I was not looking for an expert to mow my lawn perfectly. I was more looking for someone who would simply do the job every week, and more importantly, save me time so I could do the things I really wanted to do.

So from the lawn care company perspective, they might not be selling landscaping or lawn care services. Rather, they should be selling a convenience.

So what is it that you try to sell to corporations? What business are you in?

In my years in supplier diversity, I have met a lot of IT staffing companies. Because there are so many of them, our buyers are sick and tired of hearing about another IT staffing company. Even though some would tell you that they are in the "IT consulting" business, most are in the "IT staffing" business. Most of these companies use the same business model, the same sales pitch, and many actually use the same list of consultants. As a result, many of them are struggling in recent years, particularly during the recession.

The standard pitch was that they provided the most experienced people with the best price. This directly resulted in commoditizing the staffing industry. When we look at IBM, SAP, and Accenture, they might be providing the same, but they approach their clients very differently. The customer pays a premium for the same kind of people.

Some companies provide services in managing projects. Undoubtedly, these companies come and present how experienced the owners are in managing projects or how impressive the credentials of their project managers are. This approach created a few problems. For one, the company is just one of many that provides project management services. Two, this encourages the customer to look for an expert project manager with cheapest price. In addition, are the corporations looking for the best project managers in the world? In reality, people in most major corporations are probably good project managers, and their challenges are not a lack of expert project managers, but a lack of time to manage many projects and the need for peace of mind.

Once a friend of mine was on an initiative to find a company to be general contractor for a high profile construction project. A MBE did a great job in presenting their capabilities including a great process and an impressive technology platform, which the major corporations did not have.

At decision time, the team agreed that the MBE probably could manage the project. The question came to this: with many things the project director needs to worry about with such a high profile project, does he need to worry about this construction piece? Which company would give the team a peace of mind and not have midnight phone calls? This is not to say that the MBE only talks about the "peace of mind" during the presentation. If the MBE believes their business is in providing "a peace of mind," their capabilities and expertise in managing projects will be naturally only one part of the offerings.

To get your business ready for Corporate America, you need to have a clear understanding of what business you are in and position it correctly. Look beyond your products and services and see the values you offer to your customers, and the experience and feeling you create for your customers when and after they use your products or services.

Tony Hsieh, CEO of Zappos said that "Zappos is a customer service company that just happens to sell shoes." What business are you in?

Get Yourself Ready Mentally

Raymond Davis owned a printing business. One day I saw him at a trade show, and he was very excited to share with me his success. "I finally got a RFP [request for proposal] from BigCo," he said. Then he asked, "Do you know how long I have been working on this prospect?" And he answered himself, "Five years. In the past five years, I have been persistent, getting to know the buyers, and making sure they know me and what I do. I don't know yet if I will get the contract, but I am hopeful."

From my years in corporate procurement, I have met thousands of small business owners. Each one of them was eager to do business with big corporations. With the name recognition, credibility, revenue, and profit, MWBE spend precious resources (thousands of dollars and countless hours) to attend tradeshows and conferences in hopes of meeting buyers who will give them a contract on the spot. Many are very persistent and keep trying again and again. But a contract on the spot seldom, if ever, happens. Doing business with corporations is a time-consuming, brain-draining, and spirit-killing journey. You better be ready mentally before you embark that journey.

First, the sales cycle is long. Corporations are in business for a long time and they have contracts in place for almost all the categories, and these contracts are normally multi-year contracts. In addition, even the contract is about to expire, the corporate buyer is in no hurry to change vendors unless the incumbent is not meeting the corporation's needs. If you are lucky and a RFP is issued on the spot, the performing incumbent always has an upper hand. The incumbent has the relationship, knows the people, and most importantly knows the requirements, which in some cases they have helped draft in the first place.

To me, the right timing is not when an RFP is issued. Rather it is at the point that your potential corporate customer is one to two years away from the expiration date of the existing contract. This is the right time for you to build the relationship, understand the customer needs, and most importantly, educate the prospect about what you have done and what you are capable of doing. Thus, your sales calls during this period are not rushed, nor do they make or break a deal.

Second, the decision making process is long at corporations. They have to meet minimum bid requirements, sometimes high-up executives have to approve, a number of people have to meet and agree on the selection, and finance has to perform due diligence. Sometimes the buyer has to check references. All these activities have to take place and take time.

The long sales cycle can be frustrating. In addition, the corporate customers demand products or services on a large scale. If you have been working with customers only in the local city or state, now you have to service nationally or even globally, that can be mind-boggling. Global customers have other challenges: time zones, distance, technology, language, and culture. These challenges will add additional stress on you and your business. For example, if you get a national contract but your presence is limited to a few states, you will need to invest in the territories where you don't yet have a presence. If you don't manage right, your business will suffer.

Are you ready to invest in the long process in order to get a big contract with a major corporation? Prepare yourself well in advance. Always remember why you decide to get into this corporate marketplace – and have a good plan to deal with possible challenges on the way.

Get Your Management Team Ready

Ten or so years ago I was invited to speak at a local chamber of commerce for minority businesses. I was talking about how to sell to corporations and government agencies. One of the business owners followed my suggestions to get certified by a local minority supplier development council and by the federal government. The next thing I learned was that he successfully landed a big contract with the U.S. Army supplying them with PCs to support the war effort in Iraq. So one evening at a dinner function, I saw him constantly going out of the room. When I got a chance, I chatted with him briefly asking him about this business. He complained that he never had enough sleep. With the time difference, he might have to answer calls late night or early morning to service the Army in Iraq; during the daytime, he had American customers to service as well. He said, "My business is growing and my life, shrinking."

Doing business with big corporations can be very rewarding and a big boost for your revenue, if you have the capacity to service them. And that is a big if. You cannot be a one-man show and execute a large contract with a corporate customer successfully. When you make the decision to go after the big fish, you'd better start building your management team first.

A typical management team consists of a number of key positions such as chief executive officer (CEO), president, chief operating officer (COO), and marketing vice president. It is expected that a small business may not be able to afford a complete management team, nor may it be necessary. The key point is to make sure that the customer's needs are met and that you, the owner of the company, also have a life. Therefore, the most important must-have is an executive who manages the day-to-day operation for you. It is the COO, or general manager, or president, whatever title makes sense to you. Your COO will manage the day to day operation for you so that you as owner and CEO can have a life and strategically plan the future of your business. Consultants like to say, "You need to work on the business, not in the business."

For someone to succeed as a COO, she needs to have experience in the industry and have demonstrated that she can make things happen and get things done. The other criterion is that she needs to have experience managing people. Even when the right person is hired or promoted, your job is not finished. You need to have a meeting and establish expectations for both the COO and yourself. What does each of you want to get out of this new position? How do you plan to handle the differences in managing the operation? Where are the accountability and authority boundaries?

When you hire or promote senior executives to be vice president or COO, you must establish management control systems. How do you know or make sure that the COO manages the operation effectively and efficiently? You also need to have financial control system in place to minimize opportunities for someone to embezzle or damage the company financially.

A word of caution. When you have a president or COO in place to manage the operations and the corporate account, you cannot just disappear from the scene before or after you get a corporate contract. You will continue to build and expand your personal relationship with the corporate customer. For one, you demonstrate your commitment to the corporate customer by paying close attention. For two, your connections will provide checks and balances on your management team. Third, your connection with the corporations will help you generate ideas for better products and services. Particularly, after you get the contract, you need to maintain your personal touch which may be your great asset and competitive edge. Don't lose that.

Get Your People Ready

Daniele owns a small office furniture company. She has an installer on staff, but employs a few contract laborers to help set up desks and chairs when needed. In the past, a large order would be about $50,000. Then she received an order of $500,000 for a variety of furniture including conference room tables and chairs, office desks and chairs, and bookcases. Certainly the staff installer was overwhelmed and could not manage the scale of the project. Fortunately, the BigCo buyer understood the challenges. The buyer invited Daniele and her installer to visit the offices and conference rooms where the new furniture would go, and helped Daniele to determine the number of installers needed to complete the project on time. That half-a-million-dollar project went with no problem at all, and subsequent orders were also successful with added full-time installers.

When selling to large corporations, some small businesses have little idea about the inordinate and constant demand that the large corporate customer has. Big corporations have big demands, and they usually provide those with very tight deadlines. Many small businesses receive contracts with big companies, but fail to deliver at the end because of lack of preparation to meet the extravagant demand of the big business. To be successful, small businesses need to make sure that all employees are ready to sell to corporate customers and, more importantly, are ready to service big orders of the corporate customer when the contracts are signed. Let's face it: not many people are as lucky as Daniele in dealing with big corporations!

When you have set the strategy to sell to corporate customers, you need to have conversations with your employees. Explain why the company needs to sell to corporations and the benefits to both the company and to the employees. Also explain what is required of everyone for the company to be successful in marketing your services or products and in servicing the future corporate customers.

First, your employees and particularly your sales people need to be mentally prepared for a long sales cycle. They cannot expect to win a big contract at a tradeshow or overnight. Other employees need to be prepared as well, committing to the strategy long term by keeping a positive attitude and building relationships with potential corporate customers.

Second, doing business with big corporations may require a different business structure. Servicing a small order with a medium-sized business may require only one person, but servicing big corporate customers will require multiple people who may focus on separate pieces of the order. Your employees need to learn how to collaborate with each other to achieve a single, common goal.

Third, your people may need to be willing to start small at first with big corporations. One time I invited a company in a different state to bid for a small contract. I never received a proposal from the MBE nor did I receive an explanation why they decided not to bid. A couple of years later, I saw the owner of the company at a conference. He was complaining to me that he never got a contract or even RFP from us. I said we sent his firm an RFP but never heard back from them. He made a call right on the spot and his sales person confirmed the RFP but said that was a very small contract so he did not bother to work on the proposal. The problem was that we purposely made the scope of the contract smaller than it should be so as to try out one or two small MWBEs. The owner understood it, but his sales people did not. As a result, his company not only lost an opportunity for a small contract, but also lost opportunities for future big contracts.

Similarly, if you receive a small order from a large corporation, you need to service it as if it were a huge contract. You can use this small contract to test your process and system to make sure they work effectively. You can also use this opportunity to train your people on how to service big corporations. In another word, the small contract was your opportunity to demonstrate that you are ready.

Getting your people ready also means that they are technically ready. If you are in the business of managing projects, for example, make sure you have people with PMP credentials, otherwise you lose credibility before you even start talking. Yes, people without PMP designation can be excellent project managers, but the designation would be necessary to demonstrate your expertise. Similarly, if you are in the construction business, you need to have people on staff with LEED certification.

So before you set out to sell to the big companies, make sure your people are with you and ready.

Get Your Technology Ready

A few years back, BigCo had an RFP out for managing strategic events including incentive trips for sales people, user conferences, and executive retreats. The incumbent was a woman-owned business.

More than 20 companies (many were certified MWBEs) responded to the RFP including the current supplier. After reviewing the proposals, the list was reduced to 10 firms including the incumbent. A set of follow-up questions on pricing, insurance, and other things were sent to these 10 companies, aiming to further screen down to three to five firms for face-to-face meetings. The process went smoothly and one month later, a decision was made and the incumbent was replaced with a different MWBE.

About two months after the change-over, the BigCo's supplier diversity coordinator got a call from the former incumbent (WBE) asking why she was replaced. After looking back his notes, the supplier diversity coordinator told her that she did not respond to the second round of questions and all the emails and voice mails. "We thought you were either not interested or closed your shop," he explained.

The WBE said, "Oh, I am sorry. I was vacationing in Spain that month."

Technology seems to play an ever-important role in business. Fifteen years ago, it might just be cool to have an email address on your business card. Today, if you have not built an interactive, e-commerce-ready website for your business, you may not be able to compete at all.

To be ready technologically, you must have a well-designed website. Your website not only serves as your main information portal, but must be an essential part of your business. As a buyer of many services, before I send my RFP, I always google to see who is able to provide the product or service. If you have a good web presence, the playing field is leveled between you and the current supplier. However, if you don't have a good presence on the web, you may have lost the contract before the process started.

Your website needs to provide the essential information for your business, your capabilities, customer testimonials, and your differentiation, and if possible and relevant, some free resources such as white papers to educate the reader about your capabilities. This can help you convince the reader that you are a thought leader in this space. Once they are convinced of your approach, you are ahead of many competitors.

The other day, I went to a Verizon store and found that it was almost impossible to buy a "non-smart" phone. You need to set up your phone so that you are constantly connected and you don't lose a contract because you are enjoying life on the beach.

More and more companies are now actually conducting business online so a website is an integral part of a normal business process. The web-based business process includes order processing, order tracking and status updating, making inventory visible to your customers or vendors, and receiving payment. You need to have such a portal ready for business. One time I was told by a vendor that if we could give her six months and guarantee of $1 million in business, she could build such a portal. But how many companies would give you that sweet deal while other companies, MWBE or not, have already built such a portal?

A related but not insignificant issue is that your employee should not use personal email addresses to respond to emails or requests for information. You, as a company, need to be aware of the communication with current or future customers. You also need to build a system so that when an employee leaves your firm, all his customers or future customers are notified and relationship is not interrupted because an employee leaving your company. With personal email addresses, this becomes impossible. Another issue about email is that you need an email address that has your company name in it. Try not to use businessowner@gmail.com or businessowner@aol.com. Your email is also part of your marketing effort – the more people see your company name, the better.

Globalization impacts every company, large or small. Today it is absolutely required that each supplier has a non-interrupted web service.

If you are interested in servicing global companies like most multinational companies, you must be able to provide continuous service even during a natural disaster in your backyard.

Technology is part of our business operation today. Make sure you are ready.

Get Your Finance Ready

Ultimate Premium provided promotional items in the Southeast. Company owner Gary Johnson had been in the industry for practically his whole life. He founded the company in 1998 and enjoyed steady growth in the first 10 years. His clients were a mix of big and small companies, but the largest customer, BigCo, represented about 60% of his total yearly sales. His customers, small or large, were very good to him, paying the bills according to the terms (30 days for most customers). With a steady flow of revenue and very small accounts receivable, Gary's firm had no debt and he did not see the need for a credit line.

This latest recession was very tough for everyone. Some of his small business customers had to fold, and business got slower even with the large corporations Ultimate Premium retained. By late part of 2008, Gary had built up an inventory, which was lower than that during previous months. In December 2008, his largest customer, BigCo, which had a lion's share of total business informed him that as a company policy, they had to extend the payment terms from 30 days to 120 days. Gary immediately went to a few banks asking for a line of credit. In that environment, no bank was loaning money. Unable to gather enough cash flow to meet payroll and pay his suppliers, he had no choice but to fold his 10-year company.

Many business lessons can be learned in this story, but the most critical is that in business, cash is king. A big contract from a big name means nothing if you don't get the money into your bank fast enough to pay your suppliers and employees.

When you desire to do business with big corporations, make sure you are financially ready. Today, it is rare to see 120-day payment terms, but it is not uncommon to see 60- or 90-day payment terms. What happens if your customers have to change the term with you? Are you ready to weather the storm?

To be financially ready, first you need to put your finances in order. That is, follow the generally accepted accounting rules to do your bookkeeping and put in proper financial control. For example, few years ago, one MBE lost a large amount of money because one executive wrote a few checks to himself. With proper control through checks and balances, this would not have happened. Yes, you may put that person in jail, but you might never see that money again.

Second, you need to understand the true cost of doing business. Many times I have seen MWBEs quote a price that is so low the buyers get skeptical – they think that the MWBE either does not know what he is talking about or is going to lose his shirt and cannot sustain the contract. So you need to know exactly what it costs you to provide the product or services. Remember that it will also cost you money if your customer pays you later – for you have to borrow money to pay your suppliers and employees. That's why they say that money is not free. The cost of doing business includes both direct and indirect cost. Direct cost are the amount you pay to your vendors or people on the project. Indirect costs are those items like rent for the office and office supplies.

In addition to be clear on your actual cost, you need to set a target for profit margins– how much money you need to make in order to sustain your own business. Then you would know precisely how far you can go in lowering your prices. More importantly, you would also know where you have opportunities to lower your cost.

Lastly, to be financially ready, you need to have a revolving line of credit with one or more banks. You don't have to use that line of credit, but it will give you a peace of mind. It is important to get that line of credit when you don't need financing. They say, it is the easiest to borrow money when you don't need it. When you are in need, banks will think you are too risky for them. If Gary had a credit line that was big enough, he might be still in business today.

Have Your Supply Chain Ready

Lucy Gibney (www.drlucys.com) used to be an emergency room doctor and she quit her job to make and sell allergen-free cookies few years ago. In 2009, she was selling about 30,000 cookies a week. Then the real breakthrough came when she signed a contract with Starbucks. Her sales immediately jumped to 375,000 cookies a week. It was possible because prior to the Starbucks contract, Lucy had been growing her business through specialty stores and big name supermarket chains across the country. When the order from Starbucks came, she had to increase her production capacity twelvefold, production efficiency by automating operations, warehousing capacity, and triple her workforces within a year, but she was prepared enough to do so.

A supply chain consists of every step in your business from raw material to manufacturing to delivering to product returning. If you provide services such as marketing or IT, you also have a supply chain. When you decide to sell to the corporations, you need to be very clear about what your supply chain looks like now and how your supply chain may compete with those of other companies.

For example, in the promotion premium industry, the main cost is for the items that you buy from the manufacturer. When you sell to smaller companies, the number of items you need to buy may be relatively small, say no more than a hundred. So it might not make much difference if you source these 100 items from one of the few largest wholesalers in the United States or buy directly from the manufacturer. When you sell to big companies, one order can be in the tens of thousands. To be competitive in pricing, it might be better for you to source directly from a low-cost country. In addition to the pricing advantage, you may also benefit from the relationship with a manufacturer which gives you opportunities to learn what is possible in terms of design.

When sourcing from overseas, delivery time and cost can be a significant factor. But in most cases, this time requirement is exaggerated. Normally, it would take four weeks from manufacturing to delivery at your doorstep. It could save a lot of time when you buy from the wholesalers in United States if the items you order are in their inventory. If you need to customize the design, the big wholesalers might not save you much time at all for they would order the items from Vietnam or China.

Certainly sourcing from the Far East can save you time if you outsource development work such as IT, design, tax preparation, and legal research because of the time difference. The biggest success story is in outsourcing staffing. When you receive a job at 5 p.m. in New York, your partner in India can review resumes while you and your customers are asleep. When you wake up the next morning, the candidates' resumes are already in your inbox for you to schedule for interviews. This does not only lower your cost but also increases your speed of service.

Some people mistakenly think that they don't need to have a whole process worked out across their supply chain. A few years ago, an MBE received a contract from BigCo for contingency workers in a large area of the country. He did not have a presence in one of the states so he partnered with a local staffing agency for outsourcing. Without working out the whole process with the outsourced agency or communicating the requirements to that agency, the owner of the company with the contract failed to provide the necessary services. The customer had to incur a significant cost and take back the whole contract.

Today one big piece of your supply chain is your online portal. As we discussed earlier about technology readiness, you need to ensure that your online service is not interrupted because there is a natural disaster in your city or state. Fortunately, you have a number of inexpensive options through outsourcing your web hosting to Google or Amazon or other companies or to having backup services in different cities or countries, or a combination of these approaches.

When I say that you need to make sure that your supply chain is ready, I am not advocating that you hire all the people and lease a big warehouse in anticipation of a big contract with a multinational company. Instead, I simply suggest you work out the whole process and your supply chain. You need to be able to demonstrate that readiness by showing your experience in sourcing directly from a supplier in China, and in delivering products or services 24/7 and during disastrous times, for example. When the big order does come, you are ready to move forward and win big.

Get Your Product and Service Ready

Dr. Sarah Jones was the principal of a training company. Her firm could facilitate many different training programs such as management skills, emotional intelligence, and leadership coaching. They even owned intellectual properties for some programs. She had never needed to do real marketing, for all of her firm's business came from personal referrals. Her customers loved her for the quality of program content and facilitation. But Sarah had challenges to expand her business to major corporations. When they met her at conferences or events, she was always effulgent and passionate about the programs her firm could deliver. As a follow-up step, corporate buyers would ask for a brochure of her various programs. Sarah had to send out electronically after the events, and her MS Word documents were often not formatted consistently. With all of her business coming from personal referrals, Sarah wasn't interested in spending money for professionally developed program brochures.

We all know packaging of a physical product is critical to success in the retail stores. In many cases, a product's package costs as much as the product does itself. How about non-tangible product such as consulting services or training programs? The packaging of these products is equally important, because corporate buyers and business managers are used to professionally produced company and product brochures. When you present an ill-formatted Word document, people will discredit your firm and your services. So before you sell to your big corporation customers, you need to package your products and services so that they attract people's attention and draw them to your company.

The process of packaging your services is similar to that of packaging a physical product. Here are few steps you can consider.

First, know your product. What are you selling? Are you selling a training program, a consulting service, or both? What problems do your services or programs try to solve? What are the target end users of your programs and services? What are your target markets? How are you planning to offer that service or program? If you will be using people other than yourself and your own staff to do the work (facilitating training or consulting), how do you plan to assure the same quality consistently? How do you plan to deliver the services? Provide customized training on site or offer standard public workshops for everyone? License your products and train the corporations' own facilitators to deliver? What values do you bring to your customers? These and many other questions have to be answered first, for these answers impact your product packaging directly (content and format).

Second, compile the content. Much of the content is in the answers to those questions above. You will also need to prepare customer testimonies or endorsements. Prepare your current and previous customer list. In many cases, you need to spend time asking for permission to list your customers in your brochure.

Third, once you have the content ready and you are clear what you are selling, you need to engage a professional designer for the package. If you are very good in designing brochures, that's great; if not, a professional designer can make your brochure appealing in both appearance and content. This step does not necessarily cost a lot of money. Some printing shops have designers on staff. You can also try virtual designers through websites like elance.com or freelancer.com, where you can engage professional designers from any part of the world for a fraction of the cost. A word of caution with these web sites, though. You can get your brochure designed with less cost, but you will need to spend more time to get used to work virtually and to make sure the design is uniquely for you and meets your needs.

Once you engage a good designer, make sure that they are clear about the specifications the printer needs. These specifications include file format, graphic format, and color scheme. With that, your printed brochure will look exactly the same as on the computer monitor.

Please note that a good brochure does not replace your face-to-face connection and selling. Don't just send your product or company brochure through email or USPS and hope someone gives you a contract. You need to sell your products and services, and your brochure is one of the tools you need.

Get Your Marketing Machine Ready

Dr. Julia Reynolds was owner and CEO of a company specializing in diversity training. BigCo had a RFP out for a service provider to provide diversity training for the whole enterprise. The contract was significant - big name customer, millions of new revenue, and potential to expand the business into other countries. Julia's firm was invited to do a virtual presentation using the tool the corporation provided. A virtual presentation would be perfect, saving travel cost for her company and she could do the call with the co-owner and president of the company while he was in the office and she was traveling. Julia was very confident that her firm had the capability and capacity to do the job. At the web conference, somehow there was technical difficulty with her presentation's sound and her voice would disappear sporadically. She had to switch the presentation to the president, but he was not as familiar with the deck she had put together. As a result, the presentation was not as smooth as she would have liked and she had a bad feeling that she would not get the contract.

By now you are clear what business you are in and what you are selling. You have solid product or products ready, and you have marketing materials professionally designed and produced. You are ready to market to your corporate customers. How are you going to do it?

The title of this section is about your marketing machine. What is your marketing machine? Do you have one? Every company should have a marketing function, though not necessarily a marketing department. For small companies, the principals should develop a marketing plan and mobilize the whole company to execute.

The largest marketing asset of your business is your people. Everyone in the company should be trained on your company culture and values, what the company's core business today and tomorrow, and what products and service your company provides, and how it provides them. Everyone represents the company and everyone is a salesperson for the company. A few years ago, I was working on a project for a major beer company in the United States. Our project team arrived in the city for a plant visit the following day. Before the group dinner with the hosting team from the beer company, our team headed to the bar. A couple people ordered their favorite beers that were not made by the hosting company. When the people from the beer company came to meet us and saw that, they were not happy and officially complained to our project leader.

In contrast, when I met with representatives of MWBEs, I often heard them referring the companies they worked for as "they" or "them" not "we" or "us." I knew that these companies had not done the job in training their employees to represent their companies properly and not mention selling products or services. Everyone in the company should be clear about what the company is all about and who the target customers are. Thus, whatever they do, they are aligned with the direction of your company.

Today a big part of your marketing machine is social media. Facebook, Google+, Twitter, Pinterest, YouTube, and LinkedIn are tools for small businesses to gain attention on the web. The recruiters at corporations look for their candidates on these outlets, and corporate buyers also look for information about your business on the web. Creating a profile is relatively easy, but it is much harder to have a look and feel consistent with your website. Even harder is to update these profiles regularly, no less than weekly. Nothing is more discouraging than seeing your company information that is two years old!

Social media is a double-edged sword. On some outlets you are not there but people are voicing their views and opinions without your knowledge. One important part of your marketing machine is to have a way to check what others say about your company. This is true particularly if you provide services to a large number of people. Yelp and Foursqure are two platforms where people leave comments in the moment.

The third part of your marketing machine is tools for you to conduct webinars. Every day I receive information about free webinars. Most of these free webinars are conducted by service providers who partner with a major outlets like *Training Magazine*, Corporate Executive Board, and Citrix. Even if you are not interested in providing free webinars, you should have a tool like GoToTraining or Webex ready and develop the skills to use these tools. If you're not already, you will not be able to run virtual sessions either for training or for meetings. Apparently, Julia was not familiar with the tool BigCo was using or did not have prepared for the technical difficulties, which directly impacted her chance to win business.

Get Your Elevator Speech Ready

A few years ago, I was in San Francisco attending the WBENC annual conference. At the reception, I ran into Karen Herbert, an entrepreneur. We introduced each other and she told me her company was called Oya Group (www.oyagroup.com). I asked what Oya did. She simply said, "We help our customers tell their stories so that their customers remember." I applauded her wit about coming up such a succinct sentence and we had a great conversation. As of many years later, I can still remember the conversation.

I use the term "elevator speech" loosely. Many people suggest that you need to develop a statement that you can explain your business in 60 seconds. My take on the elevator speech is more about raising the listener's interest and having a conversation.

Over the years, I have met many MWBE owners. Many of these people would have hard time to explain what their companies do. They would say, "We are an IT company," "We do promotional items," or "we do staffing." When people are asking you what you do, your objective is to continue the conversation. When you say that you are an IT company, it immediately finishes the conversation. We all know too many IT companies and we think we don't need another IT firm or staffing firm. As a result, the conversation changes to something else or someone else.

Occasionally when I prompted them for more they would say, "We do IT staffing, consulting, project work, and application development. We also do data mining, web portals, etc." This presents another problem, that is, people don't remember you, because that sounds you are jack of all trades and plus, there are millions of other companies doing the same thing.

Oya Group is in the storytelling business. I just like their headline, "We help our customers tell their stories so that their customers remember." I have used it as an example for many times in my presentations and discussions. This statement has many characteristics of a good elevator speech.

First, it clearly states the core competencies of the firm and it tells us what the company does: marketing communication.

Second, it tells the listener how they do their communication work. They focus on storytelling. They believe that people love to read stories and remember stories much better than simple facts or information.

Third, it also clearly differentiates the firm from any other companies in that industry. There are tons of companies and agencies in marketing, communication, and public relations. By focusing on their specific approach, they clearly set themselves apart from everyone else.

Fourth, it also clearly states who the end customer is in their business transaction: the customers of their clients. These are the real customers in the business because if they don't get the message that Oya Group helps to craft, Oya's business is not sustainable. They are doing very well over the years and business is growing. That is a testimony to the effectiveness of that clear focus.

Fifth and most importantly, it prompts the other person to ask you questions. "How would you do that?" This would give you an opportunity to explain in more detail your approaches, your customers, and what you have done for them.

I know a women owned company in Georgia that sells office furniture. They used to have a tag line, "We furnish your space." Not bad for a short tag line. It does tell us what they do. After attending a marketing class, the owner changed that tag line to "We furnish your success." This is even better – tells what they do and raise people's interest and emotions in wanting success. It is a great conversation starter. The only problem is that it sounds cute, but it does not naturally differentiate well, because any office furniture companies can use it. From this example, we know that you must have unique capabilities and unique approach first.

So what is your conversation starter, your elevator speech?

Approach BigCo at the Right Time

One time I got a phone call from an owner of a minority business. On the phone, the gentleman asked about our IT staffing contract. I told him that we just renewed the contract with the existing suppliers for two years. He said: "That's OK. I will contact you again in two years."

When is the best time to initiate contact with your corporate prospect? Many people think the best time is right before a corporation issues a Request for Proposal. This is a wrong approach. The right initial contact would be when a contract is in place. When a contract is not up to bid in one or two years, this gives you a great opportunity to strategize and get ready for this contract when it is up for bid.

First, people do business with those they know. How does the buyer decide whom to send the RFP? Two types of firms will receive the RFP. The first group will be those he knows about either through personal contact or referral from others. The second group of suppliers includes those on the local minority or women business councils or internal supplier diversity databases. I dare to say that it is rare for someone without prior relationship to succeed in winning a contract. So to increase the odds of winning, you need to build up relationship before the RFP is issued. When someone gets the contract, it gives you a couple of years to build the right relationship with the buyers, supplier diversity managers, business managers, end users, and the company.

Similarly, buyers and business managers at BigCo will also have time to get to know your company and your capability. This can be significant if you position your business right. At least, BigCo understands that there are other equally or even more qualified MWBEs out there, and it would provide them another reason to open the contract when the time comes.

Second, you can also get to know the contract specifics in that period of time. Through tradeshows and events, you get to know the on-site manager from the supplier. Through a little bit of work, you can find out the end users in that company as well. You can also purposely find opportunity to meet with them at different events, either through supplier diversity events or professional organizations.

Third, the knowledge with the corporate target and with that contract will help you enhance your business capabilities. If there is one thing that a corporation is doing and values its importance that you are not good at, you can consciously build your capability in this area, be it your overall operation, supply chain, billing, or IT system.

Another benefit of contacting the prospect long before the contract is up for renewal is that you don't have to invest a lot of resources. The owner and maybe a sales person just need to be mindful and collect the data points.

If you wait for two years and contact BigCo again then, you will have wasted a great opportunity.

If you are serious about doing business with BigCo, the existing contract with your competitors is not a barrier but an asset to you. You need to be strategic and systematic about how you approach each corporate target. You can place each of your corporate prospects on a continuum and plan your actions for each: start the relationship with one, contact the right people with another, understand the business processes with the third, and be ready for the request for information (RFI) or RFP with another.

Know How to Market

Tim used to own an IT company that specialized procurement, supplier diversity portals, and database management. One day at an Institute for Supply Management (ISM) conference, Tim had a big booth and even sponsored a reception. I asked him why he did not have a big booth at supplier diversity conferences but had such a big one here. He explained that he liked ISM conferences much better because here he could meet the buyers of his products (procurement portals and reverse auction systems). At supplier diversity conferences, he met supplier diversity managers and some buyers who most likely were not interested in his products.

When your marketing machine is in order, you need to consider the channels where you will market your products and services. Where are you going to allow people to know about you and your company? Where are you going to not only increase your name recognition but also promote your expertise and brands?

First, we all know about conferences and tradeshows of National Minority Supplier Development Council or Women Business Enterprises National Council or US Pan-Asian American Chamber of Commerce or other national organizations and many more local "match-making" and diversity-related meetings hosted by local advocacy groups. These may be good events where you get to know the supplier diversity managers and some buyers of your target corporate prospects. We will talk later about how we can maximize the impact at these tradeshows. Many MWBE businesses only go to supplier diversity-related tradeshows, but actually there are other tradeshows that are equally important. If you are in the furniture business, there are huge trade shows where furniture makers and their customers gather; if you want to sell to food companies like Darden Restaurants or McDonald's, National Restaurant Association puts up a huge conference and tradeshow every year, where you will meet not only the restaurant companies but also their customers. So don't discount these industry tradeshows.

Second, if you are in the consulting business, there are many inexpensive ways for you to demonstrate your thought leadership and expertise, and broadcast your name and brand. A blog is a must-have tool. It will bring people to your company website where you promote more and sell more. When writing a blog, the best way I have seen is to partner with name brand companies or organizations such as *Harvard Business Review* and/or leverage name brands and authority in the field. Zenger and Folkman is a leadership development company based in Utah. Drs. Zenger and Folkman are the masters in this. If you google leadership development, you will see many of their articles on the *Harvard Business Review* blog and they email their articles to all their current and future clients. Even though many experts are in the same field and have published books as well, their companies are not as well known as Zenger & Folkman.

Third, another way to get your name out is by offering free trials of your service. For example, almost daily I get emails inviting to attend free seminars of all subjects - project management, investments, training, IT products, and talent management. These 30-60-minute free webinars do contain meaningful content or new ideas, but the main purpose is to introduce their books, programs, or products to their potential corporate customers. Some companies offered even free live sessions. A few years ago, I was invited to attend a free half-day session on Four Disciplines of Execution by FranklinCovey. That half-day generated a lot of conversations. You can also offer reduced fees to potential buyers or customers.

There are many different ways to reach your potential customers, so don't stop at the diversity events.

Know Who Your Customers Are

Though there are more small businesses than large corporations, there are thousands of big corporations. In any major cities, there are at lease scores of them that can be potentially your customers. In addition, because outsourcing has become popular in the last 15 years, most of them utilize a large number of suppliers in every aspect of their business. This is both exciting and challenging for a small minority or women owned company, for your resources are limited, and resources are needed to navigate through the corporate maze. In order to crack that nut, you have to know clearly who should be your targets so that you can put your limited resources to produce results.

But how do you determine which corporation should be your target? I would suggest three top criteria.

First is your knowledge about the company, particularly your knowledge about how the corporation uses the type of products or services that you provide. For example, every company uses outside suppliers to provide temporary employees. That does not make every corporation a target for a staffing MWBE. Some corporations use a two-tier approach: They have one or two suppliers as master service providers (first tier), and these first tier suppliers engage a number of other suppliers (second tier) that actually provide temporary employees. Other companies may use a larger number of staff companies as first tier. For the first case, if you put a lot of resources to work directly with the corporation, you may not get the return you need. Instead, your target would more likely be the first tier master service providers, particularly if you are a real small company.

Second is your existing or potential relationship with the corporation. In this book, we talk about relationships. Here it is about whether or not you know the right person who either is the decision maker or can get you to the decision maker. If you don't have such a relationship, can you build it with your resources within the time frame you can invest? If the answer is negative, this should not be your target. If you are not sure, you need to make sure before flying everywhere to attend tradeshows. Having someone's business card does not qualify as a relationship.

Third is your capability to service. If you are given a contract with this corporation, can you service them? From the first criterion, you have to know the service model of the target corporation. For example, many MWBEs are in the promotional premium industry. I know all corporations large or small use these items as giveaways at functions or conferences and in their marketing campaigns. For some corporations, this category has been highly centralized. Anyone in the corporation needing to buy promotional T-shirts or key chains has to go to a website and order. If you are in this space, your capability in e-commerce is a critical core competency. If you don't have that, you cannot even qualify to bid. (This is more than just a website for your business.)

There are other criteria that you need to take into consideration. The point here is that not every corporation should be your target. Approaching business with a corporation is like investing your money with them. You have to clearly understand your objectives and your resources. This has little to do with whether you love their brands or their products.

Work the Tradeshows

Every year, minority and women business advocacy organizations put on many tradeshows. Some of them are quite large. For example, NMSDC's annual conference and tradeshow draw some 8,000 people. Some are smaller regional events, and most are very small, local events attracting few hundred people. The purpose of all these trade shows is to bring the corporate and government buyers and MWBEs together. Unfortunately, most people don't know how to work these events and therefore, at the end of day, they waste both time and money.

From the MWBE perspective, there are several things you need to consider before going to the tradeshow.

First, determine the list of corporations that you want to connect with at different levels. For some of them, you may want to start the relationship by getting to know the supplier diversity person and hopefully the chief procurement officer (CPO), etc. For others, you may want to reconnect and enhance the existing relationship (particularly important if they are your customers). Most importantly, you need to determine a small number of corporations with which you want to make significant progress. That number can be one, but should not be larger than five. Selecting the corporations to be your target prospects should not be based on a level of corporate name recognition. Rather, it should be based on the match between the corporation's potential needs and your capabilities. The reason to limit yourself to a very small number is simply about workability. If you give yourself more than five companies, you are unlikely to be able to have quality meetings with all of them.

Second, once you know who your targets are, you need to schedule the meetings. You need to know the answers to these questions: Who (or what kind of people) would be the decision maker in using your products and services? Is that person attending the conference? How can you get connected with the right person at the conference? The supplier diversity manager can help you a lot by providing you with the right information and setting up the meetings for you.

Third, once the meetings are set up, you need to prepare for them. Prepare targeted, company-specific information for each prospect. Not all companies use the same service or product the same way, and not all companies have the same business issues. One size does not fit all. You need to create messages and use case studies that are relevant to each target prospect. Otherwise, you cannot differentiate yourself from everyone else and the corporate person would think you don't know his or her business challenges.

From these steps, you know that most work needs to be done before you attend the annual tradeshow.

Fourth, at the conference and tradeshow, you will need to execute your plan and run the one-on-one meetings, meet the right companies, and do your show.

At the national tradeshows, corporate people mainly manage their own booths and attract people to them. They are not there to visit your booths. However, in some cases, your own booth may be justifiable. For example, you may have a unique product to show case at the tradeshow. Then, your approach needs to be different – you will need to bring the right people to see your demonstration. To my knowledge, this is harder to accomplish.

Work with Supplier Diversity Managers Effectively

Supplier diversity managers can be your best friend or your worst enemy. Their job is to connect you with the right decision makers at their companies. But they are human and they have their shortcomings.

When I started out as a supplier diversity manager many years ago, I believed that my job was to serve as a bridge, to connect MWBEs to the right procurement manager and decision makers. When someone told me that supplier diversity managers were not bridges but gatekeepers, I was resentful and could not understand. Then, as time went by, somehow I became a gatekeeper as well. Being a gatekeeper, I actually became a barrier preventing an MWBE to reach the procurement manager or decision maker. The worst thing was that I could decide when I was a bridge and when I was the gatekeeper.

First, a supplier diversity manager is not a superman but an ordinary corporate employee. That means they have more work than they can do, more suppliers than they can help, and more issues internal to their companies than they can handle. There are more than 11 million minority- or women-owned firms, and at least 10,000 of them have been certified and are eager to get help and to work with corporations. No matter how hard and how serious the supplier diversity manager is to help MWBEs, it is not possible for him or her to help everyone he or she meets. Then, he or she has to select a small number of firms to spend some time with and help.

Second, supplier diversity managers also rely on relationships to work with procurement managers and decision makers. In many instances, when they present a supplier they are putting their own credibility on the line. If the MWBE supplier doesn't meet expectations, the supplier diversity manager is wasting people's time and losing credibility. It would be very hard for the supplier diversity manager to bring another supplier to the business managers. Many of us learned this lesson the hard way.

If you work it right, the supplier diversity manager can be your best friend and help you navigate through the corporate maze.

1. Get to know her. Be friends with her. You can learn a lot about her company's business and challenges. That can be very helpful in formulating your presentations when you are given the opportunity. Friends help friends. More importantly, when you become a friend, they know your business better and know you better. It is much easier for them to introduce you to the right people in the organization. In addition, she can also introduce you to her friends at other corporations.

2. Help her help you. I always ask business owners to tell me what department in a corporation uses their services. That way, I know who I need and where I need to look for that person to introduce to the supplier. You can do a lot of things to help her to help you.

3. Respect her time.

4. Help her in other capacities (not her personal stuff, of course). We are all human and we thrive in working together. On the surface, one may think that is not moral or ethical. In reality, people can make the choice to help you or help someone else. People more likely help someone who has helped them in the past. If someone asked for a hand and you refused, she may not be willing to help you when two or three other people need her help at the same time. Interestingly enough, when you help the supplier diversity manager, in many cases, you are also making yourself visible and known. Plus, what the supplier diversity manager needs help with is mostly related to an advocacy organization, and that's where you need to be known anyway.

5. Leverage their expertise to help you. Many supplier diversity managers have been in the field for a long time and they, through being friends with so many successful entrepreneurs and through observations, know a lot about business. More importantly, they know what their procurement or business managers are looking for.

They can help you formulate your strategies and presentations. Let them be your sounding board. Let them help you formulate your message, particularly when you are to present to their company.

Frank Payne is the owner of PQC International, a company that specializes in project management and training. At the beginning of his relationship with Coca-Cola, he had a contract for less than $50,000. He told me that his target was $10 million. I asked how he would do that. He described his strategies for getting into engineering services, innovation, and supply chain functions. He specifically asked me to introduce him to the heads of these functions. We then strategized the approaches, positioning, and planned the meetings. In essence, he and I became one team and collaborated. Later on, when I heard that our R&D was considering to outsource a testing lab, I worked with him to get that contract, because I knew his firm could do the job.

Help the supplier diversity manager be the bridge for you instead of the gatekeeper who blocks your entry.

Always Follow Up

John Wills is owner of a Native American company, distributing plant maintenance, repair and operating (MRO) items. At a Native American business conference, he came to BigCo's booth and introduced his firm to BigCo's supplier diversity manager. After the discussion and learning, the supplier diversity manager thought BigCo's manufacturing facilities could use John's services. So he asked Mr. Wills to send him a one-page description and with that, the supplier diversity manager promised to introduce Mr. Wills to the MRO buyers at the company. Everything worked as planned. Two or three months later, Mr. Wills got his first order from BigCo.

In my 10 years in the supplier diversity field, I have met thousands of MWBE at business expositions and supplier diversity conferences. I have also given away thousands of business cards. Unfortunately, not many people would follow up with me. Sometimes, I have met someone and thought we might be able to utilize his offerings. But at the tradeshow, I saw thousands of people, and it was tough to remember who was who. So I would ask the supplier to send an email with a one-page capability statement highlighting a specific area of their expertise. I asked people to follow up with me for two specific purposes. For one, it would remind me to identify the buyer or decision maker in the related area, and second, I could easily review the page and write an introduction to the buyer. It would make a lot easier for me to convince the buyer to take the vendor more seriously. Interesting enough, in the last 10 years, the number of people who actually sent me the one page I asked for would be less than 10.

I don't know why people don't follow up. I speculate that many people like myself have a poor memory, and they just simply forget. It is excusable, I guess, for at the conference there are many potential customers to meet and to follow up with. Or maybe they don't believe that I was serious and would take action on the capability statement. Maybe they thought I was using that as an excuse only to get them off my back. Or maybe it would take too much time to prepare the capability overview. Whatever the reason, I believe if a supplier is serious enough to spend money to attend a tradeshow and conference, he should make follow up a serious step. Without following up on the leads from the conference, you cannot be successful in closing sales with potential customers.

It may well be impossible to follow up with everyone you meet at a major conference such as the National Minority Supplier Development Council's annual conference. You have to determine with whom to follow up and how.

To determine with whom you should follow up, you must do your homework before you attend the conference. Pick up a few target companies, understand what they do and what areas your expertise may be in need by the target prospects, and register at the supplier diversity databases of the prospective companies. At the conference, verify your understanding of the corporation's business, work with the supplier diversity person or buyer to identify the niche area where you can add value. Only then will you know if there is a potential fit for your expertise and on whom you should spend precious time to move forward.

When you meet the representatives of the prospect companies, ask for the next steps and how you can follow up with them. Take notes about what details they want. Within a week, send an email to the person with what they need, and again, ask for the follow-up steps to move closer to a deal.

Following up is even more important after a sales meeting.

No follow-up is not good, but too much is not good either. At one point, several people in the procurement department and I got phone calls every other day from the same supplier. It was so bad that we had a meeting to discuss how to deal with that supplier. The solution was simple, that is to refer the supplier to only one person so that not all of us "waste" a lot of time on this. But that designated person may not be the best person to help the supplier.

So if someone asks you to follow up, please do so.

Understand Your Customer's Business

Major corporations are large and complicated. They can have hundreds or thousands of products sold in many countries. It is not unusual that I meet people who tell me they loved a particular product for they thought the product they mentioned was one of ours. When that happened, it was an awkward moment for the supplier. Before you launch your sales campaign to target particular corporations, make sure you know their business. Here are a few things you need to know.

First, know what business they are in. Like you need to know what business you are in and what you sell, you need to understand what business the corporate customer is in. That seems simple, but in reality it is not. Many companies have multiple lines of business. We all know GE is a huge conglomerate. In reality, most major corporations have multiple lines of business, normally referred as business units. UPS's main revenue comes from package operations, but its supply chain and freight business is growing fast. For Microsoft, it is not just a company selling Windows or Microsoft Office. It has five separate businesses: client, server and tools, online services business, Microsoft business, and entertainment and devices. To make things more complicated, these big corporations constantly change their business model, selling a portion of their business today and buying another business tomorrow. This is important because sometimes you think a corporation is or isn't right fit for your firm and it turns out you are wrong.

Know and study the products of your potential corporate customer and also try their products. You may not like one particular product, and that is perfectly normal - for you may not be their target customer. You won't always be able to have a cake and eat it too. Similarly, you cannot hate a corporation's products, services, or mission while you want them to give you business.

Second, you need to understand the corporation's business model, or how they perform business. For example, you drink Coca-Cola every day and think that Coca-Cola makes all these beverage products. It turns out that Coca-Cola is a franchise business. It licenses to bottling companies to make and sell the finished products. In the United States, that was true until very recently when The Coca-Cola Company bought its largest bottler's North America operation. For each segment of a corporation's business, there is also a business model issue: how do they perform their activities that are related to your offerings? With the popularity of outsourcing, some companies may outsource their procurement to a third party. If you are interested in providing security guides to a corporation, they may have outsourced the whole security services department to another entity. That will impact your sales approach.

Third, once you decide which corporation would be your prospect, you need to understand its strategic focus, both for the whole enterprise and for the line of business that attracts you. For one, it provides you a sense of how important is what you can offer to the corporation. It also allows you to align your offerings with their strategic direction, giving you a leg up over your competitors.

A company's business model specifies who its customers are and how it markets to them. Understanding this will help you find where you can add value and get an entry point.

Pick the Right Entry Point

At every tradeshow, I meet many MWBEs. After a few minutes of greeting, I ask the salesperson or owner of the business about their products and services. I sometimes got a business card and other times got a detailed laundry list of products or services under the sun. After I talked who we were and what we were looking for, many would say something like, "You know what I need is an opportunity. Just give me something and I can guarantee you that we will do a superb job for you."

Many small minority or women owned companies have been trying to sell to large corporations without much success. One of the reasons is they have not effectively positioned their company's products and services. Many of them try to be everything to everyone. If their firm is an IT company, they might sell IT staffing, consulting, project management, and application development all at once to any corporation willing to listen. Some actually believe that if they offer an array of products and services, they appear to be more capable and someone eventually will take the bait. In reality, the contrary is true. If you can do everything, people would perceive you being not good in anything. Even if you are extremely good in a number of areas, the corporate customers would prefer to start with one product or service to make sure you can deliver before they buy additional services from you.

How do you decide which product or service to push to which customer?

The decision should be a very strategic one. First, you need to target the right company. Really understand their business and how they conduct it. In particular, you need to understand how the corporate customer handles the service or products that you provide. Then, you need to understand your own capabilities and be very clear where you can add value better than other companies. From that understanding, you can easily decide which products or services you should push.

After you decide which products or services you should push to that particular corporation, you will need to find the right department or person in the corporation to contact. For example, you should not try to sell your marketing consulting services to any marketing department. Don't think that "Hey, I do marketing consulting and you do marketing. So there must be a place for me." Marketing can be very complicated at large corporations. For Coca-Cola, we have many special areas within a marketing function and some marketing may not be in the marketing department at all. Many times I would ask a MWBE which department at their current corporate customer used their product or service. Then I would try to see if we had a similar department or function to make connections for them. If you know the right person at the target corporation either through industry meetings or through your research, ask the supplier diversity manager to help you connect with that person.

Meanwhile, you will need to have an open mind and open eyes. For example, one time I was talking to our events management team about a security service supplier and trying to make some connections. My thinking was that when people manage big events, they use security services. Someone who managed video production services told me that she would like to meet the supplier. I did not understand. She told me that when she has video production projects, she also needs security services for the production location and sometimes for the celebrities and senior officials.

Picking up the right entry point to push one or two of your products and services can get you into the corporate door easily and early. That would not only give the customer some comfort in working with you, but also help yourself get familiar with them. That experience can carry you a long way.

Follow the Rules of Engagement

Janice was the owner of an IT consulting firm and had done very well for many years. Her customers were mainly stable large businesses with roots in Asia. However, during the mid- to late 2000s, business was challenging for the customers and as a result, Janice's company also suffered. Janice was very well known in the communities, and knew many senior executives of diversity and inclusion at many major corporations in the metropolitan areas. Janice and her sales executives participated in many if not all tradeshows in the state and tried very hard to sell to these companies with little success. She had many meetings with diversity executives and supplier diversity managers, but somehow these relationships did not lead to any meaningful business with these companies.

For many small MWBEs, relationships with the target company are critical to helping them gain entrance to that potential customer. However, relationship alone will not work. You have to have the right relationship with the right people. Diversity executives or supplier diversity managers can help but they are not the real users of your services or products. They may not even know who actually buys or uses your services or products. Therefore, their help may really be limited. Furthermore, many diversity executives (including some supplier diversity managers) feel obligated to meet MWBEs, and appear to be very courteous and willing to help. But when the MWBE owner leaves the conference room, they move on to things that are in need of urgent attention and selling your company was not on top of their mind.

Different companies engage vendors differently. Like in the military, you have different rules of engagement for different situations. When selling to Corporate America, you have to know the different rules used by different companies in different scenarios. Some corporations have procurement departments that are responsible for and manage product sourcing for the whole enterprise, be it a national company or global company, while others may be more fragmented and source locally. That will require very different approaches. If it is a global procurement, even if the services or products are needed in one location, the global procurement manager still plays a role. Knowing the procurement manager and building relationship with him or her are very important. In a decentralized procurement situation, you will need to know the general manager in the local facility, and sometimes the GM may have local purchasing managers. So you'd better know them and build relationships with them.

Another difference among the corporations is that some companies have an absolute rule. That is, when the dollar amount exceeds a certain level, multiple bids are required and the procurement manager must issue an RFP and request three or more bids. In this situation, you have to compete with two or more suppliers. That will change the dynamics of the process and impact how you do the sales and pricing. In other corporations, this rule may be loosely defined or enforced only in principle and users or procurement managers can source products without going through the bidding process.

Corporate purchasing is rather complicated. In most corporations, different rules of engagement apply to different categories of products, services, or functions., For example, when a food or beverage company buys ingredients to be directly used in their final products they follows a lengthier and more detailed process, as opposed to when they buy supplies for their office workers. When I was trying to move an ingredient company from second-tier status to the first-tier, I ran into many steps I did not even know and finally the MBE had to give up, for the checks and requirements were just too much for him.

In Janice's case, to be successful, Janice must know how each of these corporations buys the products or services and follow the proper rules. Go beyond the diversity executives and supplier diversity managers.

Approach the Competitors of Your Largest Customer

Sarah Taylor was an account executive for a big minority-owned company. While she was visiting a major American city, she set up a meeting with the supplier diversity managers at BigCo. About 45 minutes into the meeting, Sarah arrived. She apologized and said that she was late because she had to babysit her sister's child, which the BigCo employees believed to be unprofessional. Sarah did not get the contract. Then at a national conference the following year, she came to BigCo's booth and complained that the corporation did not give her company a chance to bid for contracts. The supplier diversity manager saw her carrying many giveaway items in her hands and offered her a branded bag to put everything into the bag. Sarah refused the offer and said that she was very loyal to her customer, a BigCo competitor, and did not want to carry a BigCo branded bag walking around. In spite of continuous effort by the minority supplier, they were not successful in selling to BigCo.

Corporations actually value other corporations' suppliers. If you can sell to McDonald's, its peers would believe that you are pretty close to qualifying for their businesses as well. On the other hand, if you want to grow your business, you need to sell to other corporations. It would be easier and more cost effective to sell the same thing to different companies. The challenge is that in most consumer product companies, the competition is extensive and pervasive in everything they do. In some cases, due to antitrust laws, they cannot appear to be working together to deal with suppliers. So how well you manage this relationship will determine how well you sell to the companies that are competitors.

First, show your respect to both corporations. It is perfectly OK and expected that you respect and show loyalty to your current customer, but you cannot disrespect the potential customer unless you have no interest in selling to anyone else. It would be advisable to consult with your existing customer and let them know that you need to grow your business and plan to approach their competitors. In most cases, they would encourage you to do so, for that will benefit them as well because they like suppliers with a large customer base. When you approach the potential customer, you act as if they are the only customer in the world. To avoid the awkward scenario in the story above, you can simply use different salespeople to work with competing customers.

Second, if you want to sell to a corporation, use their products or services when approaching them. Before you try to approach to competitive customers, do your homework. My friends at UPS told me that they sometimes receive proposals delivered by FedEx. One can easily imagine where these proposals ended. Some suppliers would spend money flying on United Airlines to Atlanta to meet with Delta Airlines executives, or rent a General Motors car and drive to the Ford headquarters to discuss business with its executives. These are not smart moves in this game. Show your respect to the corporate customer and their products.

Third and probably most important: don't disclose anything remotely confidential that you have learned from your other customer. It is not ethical and may be illegal to disclose customer information to its competitors. If you disclose something to the potential customers, they not only do not appreciate the information but also gets nervous that you would do the same with their information. At most, you can say that XYZ Corporation is your customer but may not disclose what and how much you sell to them.

So dealing with competitive accounts is tough. You need to be careful and respectful. Don't make your current customer mad, nor upset the potential customers.

Know how to Respond to RFIs and RFPs

Winston & Smith is a human resources consulting firm providing training programs and assessment tools. Through an employee at BigCo, they were invited to respond to a simple RFP by answering 10 key questions. BigCo specifically stated that the format of the response was not as critical factor as the answers to these 10 questions. However, W&S still prepared a very impressive proposal within a short period of time. As a result, they were invited to present in person and demonstrate their system and capabilities.

Now that you have prepared yourself and believe you are ready to work with corporate customers in a big way, you must follow their process. RFPs or its siblings such as the RFI or request for quote (RFQ) are in most cases a required step in the corporate procurement process. However, to a small MWBE, RFPs are a double-edged sword. If you don't respond, you give up the opportunity to win; if you invest the resource and time to respond and don't win, you waste the valuable resources.

So before you get really excited about the opportunity to respond to the RFP, you need to decide whether you need to respond. Consider these factors to help you make that decision.

First, if the project scope is aligned with your capabilities and strengths, it is a good sign. If the requirements are not in your core business, you need to pass because there are many companies that can provide those services or products better and cheaper than you do.

Second, if the corporate customer is willing to replace the incumbent or add additional suppliers, your chance of winning is better. Unfortunately, many times when corporations issue RFPs, they are simply trying to make sure that they are getting the good deal or pushing the current supplier to lower prices. There are times that corporations are seriously interested in diversifying their supplier base, and want to add a minority or women-owned (MWBE) supplier into the mix, possibly to replace the existing vendor.

Third, sometimes you know your chance to win the contract is slim to none, but you may still decide to respond to the RFP. In that case, you need to be very clear on your purpose of responding. One reason for responding is to use it as a learning opportunity. Maybe your mentor in the corporate side suggests you to respond so that you learn about your weakness and strength. Maybe you want to practice the process. In addition, many times, responding to the RFP may bring visibility to your firm and win you business in the future.

If you do decide to decline the opportunity to respond, request a meeting with the person who issued the RFP. The purpose of this meeting is to explain why you have elected not to respond to that particular RFP and express your desire to work together in the future.

When you do make the decision to respond to the RFP, make sure you understand the requirements. If anything is not clear or you have questions about the scope, ask. Here the supplier diversity manager can be you ally. She cannot show favoritism to you but definitely can provide guidance. To be fair to other respondents, the answers to your questions will be made available to all companies responding to the RFP.

One of the most challenging tasks is determining the proper prices for your services or products. You must know the true cost to you in making the products or providing the services, otherwise you will bid unbelievably low or high. Either case will not serve you well.

Sometimes, there may be a second round of RFPs with more details or additional financial requirements. This round will be sent to fewer suppliers and from the responses to the second round, only two or three suppliers are invited to do a live presentation.

If you don't win, you should ask for a feedback session. In the opening story, W&S not only asked for feedback, they actually hired a third party company to conduct the feedback session. Even if you did not respond to the RFP as a learning experience, such feedback would be invaluable for your future success. It provides you with an opportunity not only to learn about your weaknesses and strengths but also to build a long-term relationship with the corporation. Typically, corporations don't want to do such feedback sessions, because they have extra work to do and have to demonstrate their process being fair or non-subjective. Furthermore, they may feel challenged. However, you can most likely arrange such a feedback session through supplier diversity managers. So make sure you ask for this session on the ground of MWBE mentoring.

Do Your Best to be Successful

With two friends, Jerry Wong started his cabinet and floor installation company some 20 years ago. Since the very beginning, Wong & Partners tried very hard to make sure every project was a success by meeting or exceeding expectations. Their main customers are developers of high-end apartment buildings and single family housing communities. So their work represent not only their own but also the developers' reputations. Their very first big project was for a brand new apartment community. Due to their lack of experience, they estimated that they could finish in three months. It actually took them nine months to finish, which resulted in a loss of more than $100,000. Instead of trying to renegotiate the contract terms, they decided to take the loss themselves. Surely, the story got told several times in the development community, and their reputation of trust and honesty spread. Today, Wong & Partners is the major player in the high end niche in the region, and produces revenue in the hundreds of millions.

Once you are awarded the contract, you must take a long-term view of the business. Don't expect to make a great fortune with it at first. Instead, your number one priority is to make sure the project is a great success. Don't cut corners. Don't raise prices. Don't increase your margins. Do whatever needed to get the job done right. Another thing to remember is to leverage the buyer. Though the buyer's job is pretty much finished after the contract is signed, she can be your strongest advocate. She wants you to succeed as much as you do, because your failure to deliver does not make her look good; if you are successful, she will be happy to claim credit for supplier diversity and business results.

Once you have your contract in hand, the job is just beginning. First, I would suggest that you have a working session with the buyer and the end user of your services or products to really understand the requirements of the project. From the RFP and the contract signing, there can be a long time delay from a couple of weeks to six or more months. Things have changed. The buyer or the end user may have learned a thing or two through the process or some new technology has come out.

When the requirements are confirmed once again and all parties agreed, make sure you have the resources to get the job done right. If this is your first BigCo job, I would suggest you have more people assigned to the project. For one, that will make sure the job is done right; second, the more people from your company who get exposed to the way big corporations function, the more those people can help you continue the success down the road.

If this is not your first corporate contract, you still need to make sure you have enough resources for this hard-won contract. Don't spread yourself too thin and have too few people to work on too many projects. Otherwise, you may end up with more contracts but fewer satisfied customers. Then in long run, you have to scale back because of losing contracts.

At major corporations, there are always adjustments due to requirement changes, legal challenges, or other reasons. Your deadline may turn out to be impossible for you to meet. If that happens, you need to be very clear with both the buyer and the end user. You need to be up front with the user about the time required for major changes and additional cost it may occur so she is aware of the progress or lack thereof.

Remember, you should play this game in a team, not alone, and leverage the supplier diversity manager and buyers to help you succeed.

Constantly Look for Ways to Add Extra Value

Norma owns an IT staffing company and has had the contract with BigCo for a few years. Then one day, she and the president of her company were called into the BigCo's office and they were informed that the BigCo was cancelling the contract. Why? Well, before the recession, IT professionals were very expensive. In 2008 suddenly there were a lot more people available for work and the price of programmers and other workers dropped significantly. The price per hour was a fraction of what it used to be. The BigCo buyer and business manager learned that some of the people placed by Norma's company were complaining that they were not paid fairly or on time and that Norma paid the people much lower while BigCo was still paying the pre-recession rate. Essentially, Norma's company racked a much bigger margin than agreed upon. Certainly BigCo people were furious and decided to terminate the contract. For Norma, a short-sighted gain for her company resulted a bigger loss of a major customer.

Once you are on track and can continuously provide quality services or products to your corporate client, you need to be very keen in adding additional value to your customer. If market conditions change and you are able to get your products at lower cost, you need to discuss with the corporate buyers and return some of the savings to the customer. This may not be much to the corporate customer, but your honesty and integrity help enhance their trust in you. On the other hand, when the market reverses and your cost is higher, you can also be honest about it and it will be much easier for you to discuss possible rate increase.

In addition, after you can manage your process and deliver your products and services smoothly, you also need to look for ways to improve productivity through reduced time or optimized processes. You need to be, if you're not already, the expert in whatever you do. Many times your customer expects you to be the expert. You can not only improve your portion of the supply process but also advise your customer on their internal process as well. Yes, you do spend time and resources to perfect your end of the line. Through the improvement of efficiency on the whole supply chain, you add extra value to the customer. At first this seems to reduce your profit, but you can increase the profit margin. In the long run, it will benefit your business more, either through a long-term contracting relationship and/or improved productivity of your own operation. If you limit your work to deliver the agreed-upon products or services to meet the customer's minimum expectation, you commoditize your own offerings and become another vendor. It is easy for the customer to replace you with someone cheaper. Instead, if you always add extra value to the customer, your services or products are worth a lot more, and it becomes harder for the customer to replace you.

Another way you can add extra value is to bring innovative ideas to the table. You may be contracted to provide one or two services or products in one category, but that does not prevent you from presenting additional ideas in other categories. For example, if you sell promotional items and you are authorized to provide small electronic devices such as thumb drives, you can use your creative capability to propose additional way to meet the customers' business needs. That is how big companies expand their business to their existing customers.

If you constantly look for ways to add value to your contract and to your customer, you will be hard to replace. Many people complain that their products or services have been commoditized. In reality, you are in the driver's seat to prevent that, and become much harder to be replaced and much more valuable to your customer.

Grow Your Business Relationship

George spent all his career working for a global IT company and was an expert in big data and data mining. After he left his employer at the end of 2008, he launched his own consulting business providing for big corporations. He met Simon, a senior IT executive at BigCo, at an industry function and got a small contract to do data mining strategy for BigCo. After the project was completed, BigCo IT was very satisfied with the results and agreed to implement some of the proposed solutions. One day, George called a supplier diversity manager at BigCo and asked her to help him get back to BigCo. Naturally, the supplier diversity manager asked, "But weren't you here? What happened?" George replied, "That project was completed and they were happy. Simon has left BigCo, and I need your help again to do more."

When you get a new contract with BigCo, most likely you have already started or built some positive relationship with a buyer, customer, or both. The contract provides a great opportunity for you to extend and deepen the relationship for future growth of your business at this corporation and many others. One big difference between small MWBE and big companies in serving major corporations is the different levels of resources. For a big company, when they get a contract with BigCo, they put in a senior executive to manage the new account and use more resources than needed for the project. This is to make sure (1) the project continues and does not get cancelled; (2) the project is completed on schedule; and (3) the senior account executive expands the relationship through meeting other managers and executives. Thus the first project may not be significant, but within a couple of years, the business can grow exponentially.

As a small MWBE business, it is unlikely you will be able to put a lot of resources onto a rather small project. But you should consider to use the same principle: using the first project as a stepping stone for more significant work with BigCo. Don't just complete the project. Extend your network and build relationships with many more people while working to complete the project. This is not unethical and doesn't take extra time. During your project work, you will have many opportunities to meet end users, procurement managers, decision makers and other related people who will have to sign off on the result. It only requires you to be conscious and purposeful, and aim for a long-term success.

Long–term relationships are built on a foundation of trust. To build trust, we must be honest and not behave like we are the only inhabitants of the universe and don't think that no one knows what we do and what the market is. Millions of small, diverse companies thrive in the United States, and any contract with a major corporation will attract a lot of envious eyes.

To start your trust-building effort is to make sure you deliver the required product or service in a way that meets if not exceeds customer expectations. You deliver what you have promised. With that in hand, the users of your products or services become your champions in BigCo. You can find out what else they are responsible for, what their other needs are, and how you can help make their job easier and more productive in the near future. That's how many MWBEs grow their small contract of $30,000 or $50,000 to the millions in two to three years.

When you have a contract with BigCo, treat that first project as a marketing opportunity. Resource restriction is real and challenging. The only way for a contract to grow is to build more relationships with more people. So when you have people on site servicing the contract, each one has to have an antenna up all the time picking up signals about your current service quality, business opportunities, and connecting with people who are potential customers.

Support the Values of the Customer

One of my first lessons on supplier diversity was taught by an anonymous minority business owner from Chattanooga, Tennessee. One day in my early years with supplier diversity, a call was routed to me. I picked up the phone and heard a frustrated gentleman on the other end of the line. He had been trying to get some business with Coca-Cola with no success. I don't remember what business he was in, but what he said stayed in my mind all the time. He said, "We black folks in Chattanooga drank Coca-Cola for many, many years. Why can't you buy something from us?" Since then, equality and reciprocity have been one of our business cases for supplier diversity.

Customer loyalty goes both ways. After you successfully land a contract with a BigCo, you will need to support your customer. The first thing you can do is to use their services or products. If you are doing business with UPS, you need to ship your packages using UPS. This applies to shipping to UPS but also shipping to everyone else (other than FedEx). If you are doing business with AT&T, you should use AT&T for your company's wireless phone needs.

If you are in the same community as your BigCo customer, you should also try to support the community along with your customer. This does not only support what they value as important in the community, but also gives you additional marketing exposure. In Atlanta, Coca-Cola is very active in the community. They are in almost all major events related to healthy living and sports. You always see some of their MWBE suppliers participate in these events along with Coca-Cola.

A few years ago, I was entrusted to chair the board of Georgia Minority Supplier Development Council (GMSDC) and was extremely honored to get wide support from their corporate members and MBEs. I knew that was more of support to Coca-Cola. At my first annual award dinner as a board chair, I started "Chairman's Legacy," a silent auction to raise money for the reserve fund. With many donations, we raised more than $25,000. I remember there was an AT&T iPhone, donated not by AT&T, but by a minority supplier to AT&T. That was a smart thing to do. For a few hundred dollars, that MBE supported the local council, pleased their BigCo customer AT&T, and built stronger connection and association with AT&T.

In today's world, big name corporations have been easy targets for many groups and issues. From child labor to sweat shops and labor abuses to obesity issues, name brand companies are in the news every day. The issues are almost always more complicated than the advocate organizations claim to be. To many, bringing the big name companies into the news either by legal actions or consumer boycott seems to be an easy way to make their viewpoints known. Certainly as a supplier to these companies, you are not expected to defend their business practices. However, it would be reasonable to expect you not to bash them without knowing all the facts.

Nothing lasts forever. Your contract can last for many years, and sometimes by no fault of your own, it runs its course and ends. The procurement manager who has been championing your business can leave BigCo onto something different, the business managers who have been using your products or services and supporting your business can also move on to something different, and new people come in who may have their own suppliers or don't know much about your capabilities or contributions. BigCo may change business strategies and decide to outsource the work or insource what has been outsourced. Sometimes, it might be because of something you did. In either case, when it happens, it is important not to burn bridges. You have been blessed with a good run. Appreciate the opportunity. Hope your business has learned a few lessons and grown. Be graceful and move on. Business is cyclical and your opportunity will come.

Leverage Your Big Customer to Expand Your Business

Jeff Lopez owns a small furniture company and has been doing a lot of business with local governments and public schools. The furniture business in the United States is monopolized by a few major retailers and it is extremely hard for a small firm to break in representing big brand name manufacturers. Then Jeff joined a formal mentoring program through the local council and was mentored by BigCo in town. As part of that mentorship, his mentor, a furniture manager of BigCo, took him to a major furniture show. His experience of that tradeshow was totally different from the past when he went alone. Big manufacturers and major retailers stopped him and even talked to him. The association with a furniture manager of BigCo was enough for him to get to know the right people in the industry and started talks to set up a joint venture company with a major retailer.

A contract with a BigCo can be worth more than the value of that contract, but you have to manage it properly. In many cases, the big companies don't like you listing them as your customer in your marketing materials. Nevertheless, if you manage it right, you can leverage that relationship to help expand your business to other big corporations. It works because in most cases, the Coca-Colas of the world believe if you are good enough for their peers (such as Proctor & Gamble), competitors (such as PepsiCo), or global customers (such as Disney and McDonald's), you should be good enough for them as well. Certainly it does not guarantee you a contract, but it raises your profile. There are a few things you can do without getting into trouble.

First, I always advise MWBEs to work with the supplier diversity manager and ask him or her to work through their legal hoops and give you permission to list them in your marketing materials as your customer. If you go directly to the legal department of BigCo, the answer is always no, because that is the rule. While the supplier diversity manager cannot guarantee every case, she can explain the importance of helping you grow your business. The chance is much better. Because the purpose for BigCo to have a supplier diversity program is to help companies like yours to grow, it makes sense to allow a MWBE to list BigCo as a supplier in their marketing materials such as brochures and on company websites.

Second, even if you cannot list the BigCo customer in your brochure, you can still hint in your presentations or marketing materials. For example, if you said your firm provided services or products to world's largest retailer or largest home improvement retailer, we know who they are; if you worked with one of the largest mobile communication company based in Atlanta, we know exactly who you are talking about.

Third, you can use the association with your BigCo to co-brand at tradeshows. If your company name is on their display or you can distribute your marketing brochures at their booth, it would be much more powerful. It is really a win-win situation, because it also demonstrates the BigCo actually has some MWBEs to brag about.

Fourth, you can ask your BigCo buyer to introduce you to her peers at other major companies. This can be your biggest win. Most buyers or procurement managers are active in the industry, and members of Institute for Supply Management, or other professional organizations. They know each other and have great relationships. If they can introduce you to their peers in other companies, it would immediately raise your profile. It would be much easier to set up meetings with the other buyers.

A word of caution though. Don't abuse that relationship. I would suggest that your contract or relationship with the BigCo buyer is an asset, you need to cultivate and develop that asset. Don't burn the bridge or even abuse that relationship. If you want to sell to BigCo's competitors, it would be wise to let your buyer know and get her OK before you spend a lot of resources to try to sell to your BigCo's competitors. Another warning is not to play your BigCo customer against any potential customers.

Partner to Grow

Supply chain globalization and supplier consolidation have become the norm of supply chain management at many, if not all, corporations. The scope of the contracts gets bigger and bigger. Particularly for companies that have business on a global scale, scopes of some contracts can be global in nature. How can small MWBEs support a global contract? One solution has been strategic alliance or partnerships.

Partnerships are good if set up and managed right. When we look at a potential partnership, we not only look at if the partnership can be certified. More importantly, we look at the potential that the partnership helps the MWBEs to grow. The MWBE cannot be simply the sales agent or fulfillment agent for the majority partner.

A couple of years ago, a majority supplier realized that supplier diversity was increasingly important in getting more and securing existing business. As a result, they set up a joint venture company with a minority owned firm. On paper, the operating agreement looks fine and the joint venture company did not pursue a minority business certification. We reviewed how the work was going to be performed if the joint venture was awarded the contract. Then, we found that the MBE partner was simply to handle the accounting, while the actual work was performed by the majority company staff members. If the Joint Venture did not get the contract, the staff members wouldn't move to the new company. In essence, the new company was not an actual entity that would go out and secure the business but a marriage by convenience.

I always look for what each partner is putting into the joint venture. I don't believe that each partner has to put in equal values to start a successful alliance. We have to look at the whole supply chain of the new business including at what stage of the supply chain each partner adds value. For example, in the promotional premium industry, a typical supply chain would include creating the premiums or even promotions, sourcing the promotional items, warehousing, and fulfilling. Let's assume that the MBE and majority firm own 51 percent and 49 percent of the joint venture. When the JV gets a contract, it outsources to the majority company one or more of the supply chain steps (such as creative services, sourcing, warehousing, and/or fulfilling) and compensates the majority company accordingly. In this case, the majority company owns much bigger share (more than 49 percent) of the business, and worse yet, this type of alliance does not help the MWBE grow the core competencies in the process. This would not be a viable or meaningful partnership for the MWBE.

I believe the whole purpose of partnership is to grow the MWBE. If a joint venture or partnership or strategic alliance is not going to do that, there is no point in doing it at all. To ensure that, the MWBE must understand the core competencies of the business and grow them as part of the deal. Then and only then the new company will be sustainable. Use the premium industry as an example. Anyone can source products from low cost countries; many companies can provide warehousing services and equally as many can help fulfill. In my mind, the core competencies that differentiate one company from another in this industry are creative design capability and information system capability. If a joint venture company uses the majority partner company for one or both of these steps long term, the JV is not sustainable to grow into a viable business. Your partnership or joint venture company must grow the core competencies of the business, which are your enduring strategic advantages.

You partner to grow your business not someone else's.

Networking to Learn

I know you may say, "Wait a minute. Isn't this booklet called *Stop Networking*? And now you are talking about networking." I have been accused of speaking out of both sides of my mouth before, but this is not one of those times. I heard many people say, if you are not networking, you are not working. It sounds catchy and has good intentions. But networking hardly equals to working and does not necessarily lead to contracts. On the other hand, networking can be productive if you have a clear purpose and work toward that purpose. One of them can be learning. You network to learn.

But the learning should be a natural outcome, not spying. To make it work, you must be genuinely interested in others and connect with them. To make connections, you need to give and take. Ask questions about their family, company, personal hobby, etc., but you will need to answer questions at a similar level. If you ask people about their family, you will need to be willing to share about your family. If you want others to share with you their business details, you need to be willing to do the same.

At many networking events, people share what they do and how they grow their business. This can be part of the formal program arranged by the organizer or informal conversations others have. Or you can even ask people you meet what they do and how they do it.

At networking events, you will meet many people from different companies and different industries. These diverse backgrounds and companies can give you insights and inspiration to break through in your own business effort. You can ask people, "What's happening in your industry?" "What are the big challenges?" Their view can give you ideas to try in your own business.

Networking events provide great opportunities to spot industry trend and help you figure out how to grow your business in the new economic reality. A few years ago, I had a conversation with Sandeep Gauba, President and CEO of Metasys Technologies Inc. (www.metasysinc.com/) and he told me that he had attended a number of events and noticed a trend in the world of outsourcing. Procurement outsourcing started with commodities and purchasing items from low-cost countries. But Sandeep noticed that people talked more and more about business process outsourcing (BPO). He was thinking to leverage his connection with India and play a role in this new space. He started organizing procurement events in India for The Home Depot. Today this has become one of his core competencies and core businesses. As a result, he launched a new company, MetaProcure (www. metaprocure.com/).

Many times I meet people at tradeshows, and they leave the event before it even started, for they did not see how they might get a contract. No one hands out contracts at networking sessions. We all know that at networking events we are supposed to meet people, initiate contact, and build relationships. We also need to treat networking events as learning opportunities. Thus, you may not get a contract at an event, but have learned and grown, which will help you prepare for a future contract with BigCo.

When we talk about networking to learn, we cannot forget using the ever popular social networks to learn. The nice thing about Facebook, Twitter, and LinkedIn is that you can post a question directly and sure enough a lot of people will offer their advices and suggestions. For example, on LinkedIn, there are tens of thousands of groups related to business development that you can join to ask and answer questions.

Apply What You Have Learned

Many advocacy organizations and small business development centers offer training and education programs to entrepreneurs for free or a nominal cost. The topics range from starting a small business all the way to succession plan and exit strategies. Most of these workshops and seminars are very relevant to the small business, and many even specifically targeted to the unique needs of MWBEs. The feedbacks from the participants of these classes are very positive. People like the content, report it is relevant, and are excited to know the information or skills. However, in most cases, when people get back to their homes and their offices, they either forget what they have learned or don't have the will to put it in use. This situation made people think, "Training is a waste of time, a waste of money."

A few years ago, Coca-Cola sponsored two classes and both were facilitated by experts in the field of branding and key account selling. At the end of both programs, we did a traditional evaluation of the programs. The feedback was extremely positive. Both facilitators offered a one-hour free consultation to any participant after the session. For the marketing facilitator, the free consulting would be in the areas of using the concepts and skills to brand the participant's business and market its products. The participant had to develop a marketing plan and the facilitator would help review and refine it.

The sales training facilitator would also provide a one-hour free consultation to using the system that big companies use to sell to major corporations. The participant would also need to start selecting a target corporation and create a sales plan. The facilitator would then review the plan together with the participant and refine the steps before a sales call or prearranged meeting.

Each class had about 30 participants representing about 25 MWBEs. Not a single person accepted the offer.

More recently, we sponsored another training session on selling skills for small businesses. The instructor himself is a business owner, who grew his business to more than $50 million in only a few years. He used his own experience to illustrate how the sales process should work. Again, he offered help to whoever interested in implementing the sales system that worked for him. Only one or two out of the 30 participants actually followed up with the instructor, and very few if any actually implemented.

Why don't people use what they have learned in training sessions? Some of us believe that the number one reason is the environment. People leave the training, be it a one hour, one day or one week long session, and immediately jump into whatever crisis is awaiting them. They deal with the issues at hand using the most comfortable way.

How can we break the old habit and old routine and start using what we learn?

Sometimes we have to jump on the belief that it will work, and just try it out. Certainly, one would say, "What happens if it does not work?" My response would be, "What happens if it works?" It will never work if you don't try. Few years ago, at one of the training sessions, one entrepreneur picked up one simple idea to hire a COO so she could focus on strategic development of the business. At that time, her business was rather small. Once that COO was hired, she completely transformed her business from one person trying to run everything herself to freeing herself up to grow the business. In a short period of two to three years, she quadrupled her business.

Training is indeed a waste of time if you don't use what you have learned.

Way Forward

In order to grow your business, Corporate America presents great opportunities and they can play an integral role for your growth. When you make a strategic decision to go after Corporate business, you will need to make a deliberate plan. First, make sure you and your company are ready. You and your associates need to be mentally ready for this long and difficult road; your products, supply chain and technology platform all need to be ready.

Once you are ready to move, study the battle field. Pick up a few corporations as target prospects. Test your readiness. Figure out the best approach to reach the corporate customers. Make the supplier diversity managers your best friends and help them help you.

Hopefully you are successful and receive a good contract. Be conscious and mindful to grow your business in that BigCo and leverage it to get more business with other corporate customers.

You have been successful. With the same determination, deliberate planning, persistent execution, and a little bit luck, you will be even more successful.

Good luck.